My Grandma's BACKYARD

By Miles
and
William Rabun

Illustrations By
Tony Moore

To order additional copies of this book, contact:
Xlibris Corporation
1-888-795-4274
www.Xlibris.com
Orders@Xlibris.com

For Kappitola Williams
Our Drandma (Yes, with a D)
Who inspired and encouraged us
to take this journey.

MY GRANDMA'S
BACKYARD
IS FILLED

WITH SO MANY THINGS TO SEE,

YOU COULD SPEND

THE WHOLE DAY

THERE

IT'S AN EXCITING

PLACE TO BE!

WHEN MY BROTHER AND I
ENTER GRANDMA'S BACKYARD
WE CAN'T WAIT TO HAVE FUN,

THERE ARE

FROGS,

BRIDGES,

FLOWERS

AND TREES,

SHE EVEN HAS A POND!

A TURTLE NAMED SPEEDY

TWO FISH IN THE POND

THAT WE CALL

REX AND FLASH,

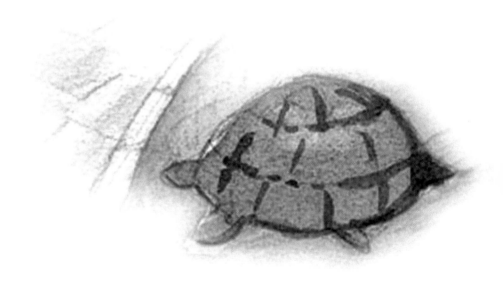

THERE ARE MANY STONES
FROM THE WINDING PATH
WE SKIP THEM
TO MAKE A SPLASH!

THERE IS A BIG WIDE STAGE

WHERE WE RECITE OUR POEMS

OR MAKE UP SKITS

AS WE GO!

WE EVEN INVITE FRIENDS

OVER SOMETIMES TO

SHARE IN ONE OF

OUR SHOWS!

SPIDER WEB PLANTS,
AND
REAL INSECTS TOO
GRANDMA'S
BACKYARD
HAS IT ALL!

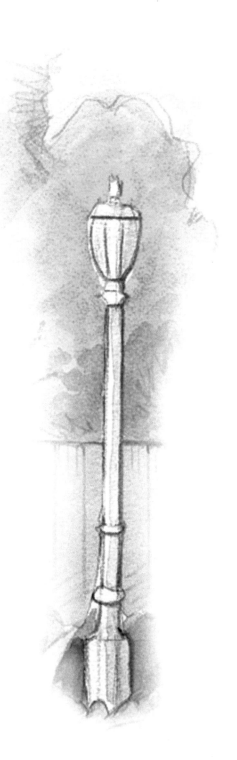

NEXT TO THE KETTLE

THERE SITS ON

ON PEDESTAL

A COOL

SHINY BLUE BALL.

EACH DAY WE PLAN
OUR ADVENTURES,
IT REALLY IS NOT HARD!

CAUSE DAY BY DAY

WE LEARN NEW THINGS

WHILE IN

MY GRANDMA'S BACKYARD!

RHYMING WORDS

The Words below have a matching rhyming word.
Draw a line to match the words that rhyme
from the story.

FLASH   BE

HARD   SPLASH

GO   BALL

SEE   SHOW

ALL   BACKYARD

WHAT'S IN THE BACKYARD?

Go back to the Story.

What are the names of the fish?

What do the boys skip in the pond?

What is shiny and sits on a pedestal?

What happens on the stage in the backyard?

Name the things that can be found in the backyard.

ACTIVITIES FOR THE BACKYARD

If you could choose your activity for playing
in the backyard, which would it be?

Skipping Rocks in a Pond

Doing Plays and Skits on a Stage

Climbing Trees

Watering and Feeding Plants and Flowers

Which one did you choose and Why?

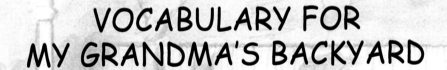

VOCABULARY FOR
MY GRANDMA'S BACKYARD

GREENHOUSE

FERN

INSECTS

PEDESTAL

KETTLE

PLANTS AND FLOWERS IN THE BACKYARD

Name these flowers or plants:

1.

2.

3.

4.

5.

6.

Can you name the plant found in the backyard in this story?

RHYMING WORDS

The Words below have a matching rhyming word.
Draw a line to match the words that rhyme from the story.

FLASH

HARD

GO

SEE

ALL

BE

SPLASH

BALL

SHOW

BACKYARD

WHAT'S IN THE BACKYARD?

Go back to the Story.

What are the names of the fish? REX AND FLASH

What do the boys skip in the pond? STONES

What is shiny and sits on a pedestal? BLUE BALL

What happens on the stage in the backyard? SKITS AND PLAYS

Name the things that can be found in the backyard.

FROGS, BRIDGES, FLOWERS, TREES, AND TURTLES

PLANTS AND FLOWERS
IN THE BACKYARD

Can you name the plant found in the
backyard in this story? SPIDER WEB PLANT

1.

Daisy

2.

Red and
Yellow Pansy

3.

Tulips

4.

Daffodil

5.

Fern

6.

Orange DayLilly